The Vending Machine Business Blueprint

An Easy, Step-by-Step System to Build A

Six-Figure Business That Prints Money

While You Sleep

Josh Hall

Table of Contents

Introduction

When you think of passive income, what comes to mind? A rental property? Or perhaps a diversified investment portfolio?

These are what I would call traditional streams of passive income—an investment strategy your parents grew up learning about. However, the world has changed drastically over the past few decades, and there are now modern ways to earn passive income that don't require a trust fund!

A vending machine business is probably not something you dream about. But what if I told you that it is one of the most lucrative passive businesses and that it has low startup costs and low overheads?

Not only does the math add up, the business model is flexible enough to be customized to your niche market. This means that whether you are selling candy or hot pizza, you will always find customers who are looking for on-the-go convenience.

At this point, you are probably thinking, "What's the catch"? The truth is that there is no catch. But like any other business, running a successful vending machine enterprise requires the perfect mix of the right product, price, location, and marketing strategy.

This short blueprint has been created to provide you with the A-Z steps on how to register a business, set up a business plan, buy the right vending machine, manage operational costs, build a reputable brand, and so much more!

If you want to cash in on the $10.2 billion industry and become a vending machine operator, this book is the perfect resource to kickstart your journey. Get ready to learn how to double your income without having to quit your 9-to-5.

Chapter 1

Why the Vending Machine Business?

Chase the vision, not the money, the money will end up following you.

–Tony Hsieh

A Snapshot of the Industry

In the US, the vending machine industry has a market value of $10.2 billion as of 2022 (IBISWorld, 2022). It falls under the Retail Trade Industry and has been ranked 49th in the industry (based on market size).

From the period 2017–2022, the vending machine industry has grown by 0.8% each year on average. However, the increase in demand for on-the-go products and cashless payment systems are just some of the reasons why the industry is expected to see consistent growth.

Growing up, you may remember only being able to buy snacks and beverages from vending machines. But nowadays, this is not the case. While snack and beverage machines continue to lead in the market, new niche products being sold through vending machines are slowly changing consumer purchasing behavior.

To put it simply, pretty much anything that can be bought with money can be sold through a vending machine. This ranges from cigarettes to beauty products, and everything in between. The ability to sell a wide range of products creates an opportunity for operators to generate a significant amount of revenue by strategically positioning their machines in the right location, with the right product.

Potential Earnings

The main objective of starting a business is to generate income. The vending machine business is profitable; however, it is important to remember that not every machine will make money, due to a number of factors such as the type and price of products, as well as where the machine is located, and if there is a big enough demand. Therefore, how much you earn has a lot to do with how your business is structured.

Nevertheless, let's take a look at the numbers!

According to VenTech Media, the average American spends $27 per year on vending machine items and the average purchase amounts to $1.75. A normal snack and beverage vending machine generates just over $75 of revenue per week, which comes to $300 per month (VenTech Media, 2020). Since profit margins on vending machines vary, not every machine will generate $300 monthly. Some may generate much less or significantly more!

The type of products you sell will also affect profitability. The more novel or in-demand your products are, the higher the profit margins you can take home. This is because consumers know that they cannot find those products anywhere else. However, if you are selling soda and snacks that sell cheaper elsewhere, you may not have enough leeway to increase your profit margins.

Startup Costs

Earlier on, I mentioned that running a vending machine business comes with low startup costs and low overheads. This is perhaps one of the most attractive aspects about the business model. Nonetheless, similar to the potential earnings, the total startup costs will vary depending on the type of vending machine you are interested in (more on this in the section below).

In general, the bulk of your investment will go toward purchasing the vending machine and stock items. The most affordable vending machines go for $300, but the fancier and more high-tech machines can reach upwards of $5,000. If you are working with a small budget, you can get your vending machine business up and running with as little as $2,000.

Please note that startup costs do not include operational costs—the monthly expenses incurred while running your business. Examples of operational costs that you will need to factor include insurance, inventory, maintenance, leasing fee, sales tax, and loan repayments.

Vending Machine Options

When we think of vending machines, we often picture the standard snack and beverage machine. However, this isn't the only type of vending machine available on the market. If you find that your area is overpopulated with snack and beverage machines, you can differentiate your business by opting for a different type of machine. Below is a list of vending machine options you can choose from.

1. Food and Beverage Machines

Machines that stock soda, snacks, and candy are known as food and beverage machines. They remain the most profitable type of machine, accounting for more than 43% of total vending machine revenue globally (Grand View Research, 2019). If you are looking for an option with the least amount of risk, then the standard food and beverage machine is the best pick.

2. Bulk Vending Machines

The most affordable vending machines on the market are the bulk vending machines. These are the miniature machines you find in malls or kids' play areas that are stocked with gumballs, small toys, or stickers. Besides the affordability, these machines require very little upkeep, which means your maintenance costs will be considerably low. The only potential drawback is the potential monthly revenue. The average monthly revenue generated by bulk vending machines is $30. The good news is that the stocked products come with extremely low overheads, so even if you only make $30, you are still walking away with profit.

3. Specialty Vending Machines

If you have a few chunks of change to spend on a vending machine, you may be interested in purchasing a specialty machine. These types of machines are custom-made to stock specific products, or to perform specific functions. Unlike food and beverage machines, it is rare to find a refurbished speciality machine because of how niche they are. Examples of specialty machines include:

- Hot beverages machines

- Electronic gadgets machines

- Luxury products machines

- Alcohol beverages machines

- Beauty and cosmetics machines

- Medication and wellness products machines

- Hot savory meals machines

- Clothing machines

- Laundry products machines

Before settling on this option, find out what items are permitted to be sold in your jurisdiction by contacting local authorities.

4. Franchising Option

The final option is to purchase an existing vending machine franchise with an established customer base and routes. The upside to choosing this option is that you are buying into a business model that has already been proven to work. Your franchisee agreement may even come with free support and training to help you get started. You will also be able to calculate how much revenue you will generate per machine, making it easier to scale your business.

One of the main drawbacks is that you don't have as much freedom to customize your brand or tweak the business framework. Moreover, depending on your agreement, you may have to pay a portion of your revenue to the franchisor periodically.

There is no right or wrong way to set up your vending machine business. Just make sure that whichever option you choose, you purchase one or two machines with a specific target audience in mind. When you have found the perfect formula for product, price, place, and promotion, you can add a new machine.

Pros and Cons for Starting a Vending Machine Business

With any business comes a number of pros and cons. This is because despite having a solid business model, there will always be factors that you cannot control. Generally speaking, vending machine businesses are attractive for first-time entrepreneurs, as well as those who are looking to build automated businesses. However, with this being said, there are still drawbacks that must be considered. Below are a few pros and cons of starting and running a vending machine business.

Pros of Running a Vending Machine Business

Here are the top reasons why you should be excited about starting your vending machine business:

1. Low Startup Costs

Starting a business requires startup capital. This initial investment can range from $100 to $100,000. A vending machine can be up and running with just a few thousand dollars to start with. Of course, as time goes on, you will incur operating costs, but these can also be kept to a minimum by, for example, leasing rather than buying a machine, and sourcing products nearby.

2. Low Risk

Since your initial investment is low, you are exposed to less financial risk. You can use the first vending machine to test the market, location, and products. When you have finally found your winning formula, it is safer to invest in a second machine and rinse and repeat the strategy.

3. Flexible Management

Many business owners are drawn to vending machine businesses because they require very little active involvement. This doesn't mean that you can completely abandon your machine, but you will only need to check on it periodically (like once every week), in order to collect money or assess security. If you are currently working a 9-to-5 job, you can set your own business hours and decide on how frequently you replenish stock.

Cons of Running a Vending Machine Business

As attractive as this business framework is, we cannot overlook the drawbacks. Here are some challenges you will need to carefully plan for:

1. Profitability Depends on Scaling the Business

One vending machine can make you break even or pocket a few hundred bucks every month. But, if you are looking to generate thousands of dollars in revenue, you will need to focus on reinvesting into your business and purchasing more machines. Note that if a single machine is making $100 per month, it will take several years before you can purchase a second machine. To accelerate the process, you can seek a business loan and pay it off in manageable monthly installments.

2. Tight Competition for Prime Locations

Vending machine operators know that being situated in the right location is winning half the battle. As a result, operators compete for prime locations, which happen to be in areas with a high population of blue-collar workers. When starting your business, one of the main priorities will be to find a spot that receives sufficient foot traffic, but isn't saturated with vending machines (or at least the type of vending machine you are looking to invest in).

3. Risk of Accumulating Expenses

The profit margins on vending machines are not high. To succeed in the business, you will need to reduce your expenditure as much as possible. Typically, operators budget for monthly expenses, but get a rude awakening when fuel prices increase, when paying exorbitant sales tax, or needing to repair the machine on a regular basis (especially if it is a pre-owned machine).

To avoid the accumulation of expenses, take the time to account for every small and large expense. Try to run your business as lean as possible, so that you have emergency funds to tap into when you are faced with a financial crisis.

Chapter 2

A Business Plan to Maximize Success

The best startups generally come from somebody needing to scratch an itch.

–Michael Arrington

Do You Need a Business Plan?

Roughly 543,000 startup businesses are registered each month in the U.S.. Within the first two years, seven out of ten businesses are still operating, but at the five year mark, only five out of ten businesses are active. What's interesting is that 70% of the businesses that make it to the five year mark follow a strategic business plan (Nazar, 2013).

A business plan is more than just a 50 or 100 page document that sits in your office and gathers dust. It is a blueprint that outlines the growth plan for your business. The purpose of the plan is to prepare your business for the journey ahead by setting out the step-by-step processes on how to achieve your goals, increase sales, and build a reputable name for yourself.

If you are planning on seeking funding, most lenders will require you to have a business plan. They will want to see your income projections and if your business model is viable or not, before approving your for the loan. Therefore, not only does a business plan increase confidence in yourself as an owner, it also increases the confidence of your potential investors.

Below are the main components of a business plan that you will need to include when creating your living document. Feel free to customize each section, adding as much detail about your business as possible.

Executive Summary

The executive summary is a one page introduction and overview of your business plan. Many people prefer to write it last since it is made up of the key points mentioned in each section of the plan. The goal of writing the executive summary is to assume that the reader will not have the time to thoroughly go over every page of the document. Therefore, present all of the need-to-know information, such as your business model, direct competitors, target customers, overview of the marketing strategy, and overview of your financial plan.

Company Overview

In this section, you will get the opportunity to introduce your business in more detail. Some of the key elements to include are the industry analysis (snapshot of the market you are entering), the company's legal structure, your vision and mission statement, as well as the company goals and objectives. If you are on top of the game and already have a company brand, this would also be a great place to share more details about it (including logos and other branding elements).

Customer Analysis

The customer analysis focuses on defining your target market and creating various customer profiles. Your goal when writing this section is to think about the people who would be most interested in purchasing items from your vending machine. Your analysis can begin broadly by creating customer segments. For instance, you might come up with two segments: people who work at office buildings and people who work at construction sites. Thereafter, you can'break down each segment and think of your customers in terms of their age, gender, income level, and needs and wants.

Competitor Analysis

Since you are not the first vending machine business in your area or the first company to sell food items, you will have both direct and indirect competitors. Direct competitors are those businesses who operate in the same market and sell similar products. In this case, these would be other vending machine businesses. Indirect competitors would be those businesses who are not necessarily competing in the same market, but operate within the wider industry. Examples of indirect competitors for a vending machine business would be traditional restaurants, convenience stores, hot dog stands, grocery stores, and so on.

For each competitor, provide a summary of their business, what they sell, as well as their strengths and weaknesses. When considering their weaknesses, think about it from a customer's perspective. For instance, what needs or wants is the business failing to respond to? The final section of the competitor analysis should include your competitive advantages, in light of what your direct and indirect competitors offer. Here are a few questions to get you thinking about your competitive advantage:

- Are your products niche or superior?

- Will you provide lower prices for goods?

- Will your service be easier or faster?

- Will you provide better customer service?

Marketing Plan

The best way to structure the marketing plan is to focus on addressing the four P's of marketing: product, price, place, and promotion. Let's briefly look at each "P" and what it entails.

- **Product:** Your product is the vending machine that you will be operating, as well as the products inside the vending machine that you will sell. Mention all of the saleable products and why you have chosen those specific items (i.e. justify why your target customers would purchase those items).

- **Price:** Record the prices for goods and how they compare with your direct competitors' prices. This portion of your marketing plan can be a simple spreadsheet with a list of product prices.

- **Place:** Describe the location of the vending machine and why you have chosen that exact location. Mention any amenities that your location offers that can support your business, such as having plug points, 24/7 security, or being situated close to a cafeteria or food court. You should also justify how your location will bring a steady stream of foot traffic.

- **Promotion:** Create a strategy for attracting customers to your vending machine. Note that there are a variety of ways to promote your services, which can include online advertising or offline signage and branding. You can also look at ways of making your vending machine more appealing, such as keeping it clean, improving machine technology, or placing the machine in a strategic location.

Operations Plan

The first few sections of your business plan explained your goals. The operations plan documents how you will achieve those goals through daily, weekly, or monthly processes. When you finally begin trading, avoid deviating from your operations plan because doing so might cost you more time and money. In general, the operations plan can be divided into two sections: short-term processes and long-term milestones.

The short-term processes include all of the day-to-day tasks that are involved in running your business, such as the sourcing of products, stocking of machines, collecting of money, and keeping the machine safe and clean. The long-term milestones include goals that you hope to achieve in the future, such as purchasing a second or third vending machine, when you expect to hire your first employee, or reaching X amount of dollars in sales by a certain year.

Management Team

Even if you don't have employees working for you yet, it is important to establish a strong management team. At the beginning, you may be the only person on the team. This is normal, but bear in mind that most of the managerial responsibilities will fall on you. Some of the information you can add to this section include your résumé, emphasis on the skills and experience you bring to the business, and an overview of your business title and duties. Feel free to also outsource managerial responsibilities like accounting or managing the operations, while growing your business and getting it to a point where you can hire an in-house team.

Financial Plan

The financial plan is usually the last section of your business plan (unless you are going to include an appendix). It typically includes a 5-year financial snapshot of your business, broken down into monthly or quarterly statements for the first year, then annual statements for the remaining years. The type of financial statements you can include are income statements (also known as a profit and loss statement), balance sheet statements, and cash flow statements.

Compiling a business plan can take anywhere between one month to one year. What tends to speed up the process is having all of your research ready. It is also helpful to carefully analyze your plans, processes, and systems before writing them down on your business plan. This will ensure minimal issues when you apply them later on. Weigh their strengths and weaknesses and compare them to what your competitors are doing or the latest trends in the market.

Chapter 3

Buying the Right Machine

*Behold the turtle, he makes progress only when
he sticks his neck out.*

–Bruce Levin

Factors to Consider When Buying a Vending Machine

Having the money to buy a vending machine is one thing, knowing which kind of vending machine to buy and what to look out for is another. It is important to remember that no vending machine is the same. Some are new, others are refurbished, and many of them vary in design and technology. Therefore, when selecting a vending machine, think about what your particular business needs are. Below are a few factors to consider when purchasing a vending machine.

1. Type of Vending Machine

The type of vending you choose will be informed by the products you wish to sell. If you are going to sell beverages, you will need to buy a beverage vending machine. Refer back to Chapter 1 and have a read over the vending machine options available to you.

2. Location

Another key factor is location. Certain types of vending machines work best in certain locations. For example, hot beverage machines do well in office buildings because of the number of people who buy hot coffee or tea in the mornings or late afternoons, whereas a bulk vending machine serving pieces of candy may do well in children's play areas. When picking a location, consider the demographics of customers in that area and what those customers are likely to purchase from your machine.

3. Easy to Use

One of the biggest advantages for buying items from a vending machine is the convenience factor; customers who are on-the-go can spend less than five minutes buying food and drinks. When purchasing a vending machine, think about how quick and easy it is to transact. The more complex the system, the less likely customers will return. In general, if a 10 year old finds the machine easy to use, then most customers won't have much trouble using it either.

4. Safety

When purchasing a vending machine, consider the safety of your customers too. There shouldn't be any injuries incurred during the buying process. As the vending machine operator, you will be held liable for any accidents involving your vending machines. Therefore, complete your safety checks, include warning labels, and make sure customers understand how to use the machine (you can add step-by-step guidelines on how to purchase items).

5. Size

The location and amount of space you have to place your vending machine will determine its size. It is recommended to measure the space first before deciding on a particular size. Mini machines are suitable for smaller spaces and larger machines work best when you don't have any space restrictions.

The Cost of a Vending Machine

The cost of a vending machine can range from $100 to upwards of $5,000. There are many factors that determine the cost, such as the type of vending machine, whether it is new or refurbished, and how modern the technology is. Buying a refurbished machine may be more affordable, however you should take into consideration the kinds of features customers are looking for.

For example, in these modern times, customers prefer cashless "pay-and-go" systems that make buying easier. Some may even prefer specialty vending machines that offer products one would typically find in a drug or grocery store. Ideally, you will want to buy a vending machine that offers you modern features, at the lowest cost. To find these gems, be prepared to do extensive research and negotiations.

Where to Buy a Vending Machine

Finding a vending machine has never been easier! All it takes is an online search. The difficulty comes in narrowing down your search and finding the most reliable machine suppliers–locally or internationally. The truth is that there is no shortage of vending machine suppliers, but not all machines are built with the same quality and standard. Never settle on the first supplier you come across; do your research and compare what you can get from different businesses.

To help you begin the search, here are three types of sellers you will find online:

1. Manufacturers/Wholesalers

These types of sellers have the widest range of vending machines (both modern and traditional) available on the market. Not only do they sell vending machines, many of them also offer additional services like repairs and training.

2. Secondary Market Sellers

Also known as specialty online retailers, these sellers have an online marketplace that gives you access to different vending machine brands and models. Some websites may even include helpful resources for entrepreneurs to successfully run their businesses.

3. Consumer-to-Consumer Platforms

Online marketplaces such as eBay or Craigslist host thousands of listings for vending machines. In most cases, the listings come from vending machine owners who are looking to sell their pre-owned machines at affordable prices. The risk of buying a machine through these types of platforms is the issue of quality. Since the machine is not new, nor was it bought straight from a manufacturer, you are not guaranteed that it is of the highest standard.

When deciding on a seller, make sure to look through the customer reviews online. Avoid sellers with less than three star ratings, as well as those who have poor customer service. Ideally, you need to look for sellers who are reliable, offer seamless delivery, and are available for ongoing support and machine maintenance.

Chapter 4

Stocking Your Vending Machine

Every day that we spent not improving our products was a wasted day.

–Joel Spolsky

Popular Items to Stock in Your Vending Machine

A crucial factor that determines your business's profitability is the types of products you sell. You might have the latest high-tech vending machine, but if you get the products wrong, your machine won't make a lot of money and it will be a bad investment. When choosing products, avoid thinking about what you would purchase, but instead consider what the majority of your customers would purchase. At the end of the day, they are the ones who will visit your machine on a daily or weekly basis, so stocking their favorite items will help you keep customers coming back.

Different customer segments will have unique vending machine preferences, but in general, here are some of the products consumers find most attractive for vending machines:

- Snacks (Snickers bars, Clif bars, pop tarts, Sun chips, granola bars, nuts and seeds, pretzels, dried fruit, popcorn, etc.)

- Drinks (Bottled water, energy drinks, vitamin water, cold coffee, soda, iced tea, etc.)

- Mini meals (Soups, noodles, rice dishes, pasta dishes, breakfast bowls, etc.)

As much as soda and snacks sell really well, more and more consumers are seeking healthier food alternatives. If your customers fit under the demographic of people who live healthy and active lifestyles, consider adding a few healthy options inside your vending machine to accommodate them.

Best Places to Buy Vending Machine Products

To keep your expenses to a minimum, it is crucial to source your products from the right suppliers. Similar to the process of sourcing a vending machine, you will need to conduct an online search. You will notice that there isn't a shortage of product suppliers in your area or abroad. However, once again, each supplier might offer different perks, customer service, and product quality. Avoid choosing the first supplier that you come across. Take your time to compare different suppliers, so that you can find one that offers value for money.

Here are the types of product suppliers you are likely to come across while doing your research:

1. Wholesalers

Wholesalers offer the widest selection of products at the lowest prices on the market. Some may give you the option of buying in bulk or small quantities, while others may enforce a minimum order quantity. Due to their large-scale operation, wholesalers are able to ship products to you from anywhere in the world. Many of them also have great return policies, like being able to replace products within 24 to 48 hours.

2. Cash and Carry Suppliers

These companies are often associated with a major wholesaler. They operate similar to a grocery store and allow business owners to buy products in bulk at competitive prices. Even though you might end up paying more for goods than a wholesaler, you won't have a minimum order quantity. One of the drawbacks however, is that many cash and carry suppliers don't offer shipping, which means you will need to drive to the store to pick up your products (this becomes an issue the farther away you live from a store).

3. Brokers of Specialty Products

There are also agents who run private distribution businesses that specialize in sourcing and selling specialty products. Most of the time, these products cannot be found in major retail stores due to how niche they are. If you are operating a specialty vending machine, partnering with an agent can help you identify niche product manufacturers to work with. Initially, the cost of working with an agent is expensive, but once you have established good relationships with manufacturers, you can cut out the middleman ("agent").

4. Membership Clubs

Membership clubs are offered by companies like Costco, Sam's Club, and BJ's. Membership is open to the general public; however, it is typically attractive to businesses looking to purchase wholesale products for discounted rates. Membership clubs operate similar to cash and carry suppliers, except you are able to buy goods at wholesale prices. Membership fees will vary for each club, but you can expect to pay about $50 annually.

When sourcing products, you can use more than one type of supplier. For example, you can source bulk items like bottled water directly from wholesalers, and seasonal items from membership clubs. The aim is to keep the costs down to a minimum, while sourcing quality products and making sure you have a wide range of products available for customers to choose from.

Chapter 5

Location Is Key

You just have to pay attention to what people need and what has not been done.

–Russell Simmons

Factors to Consider When Looking for the Right Location

Another factor that affects the profitability of your vending machine business is the location. Your goal should be to get as close as possible to your target customers. Of course, this isn't always easy since the competition in the market is already tight. You are likely to find a number of vending machines already situated in the hot spots where your customers spend a large portion of their time. Nevertheless, this shouldn't discourage you. You can still find prime locations by closely examining the following factors.

1. Look for High Foot Traffic

It is important to place your vending machine where you are most likely to get a lot of foot traffic. This is why you need to have a good understanding of where your customers are located. To have consistent sales, you should target repeat customers; those who purchase items on a daily or weekly basis. When considering location, find a spot where customers walk past on a recurring basis, such as a hotel lobby or cafeteria.

2. Study Your Competition

In such a competitive environment, you need to study and monitor your competitors to identify the hot spots. Situating your machine near competitors can be advantageous because it shows that the particular area experiences high foot traffic. With that said, too much competition is never a good thing. As a general rule of thumb, if there are more than 10 vending machines within a specific radius, look for a spot farther out.

3. Ask for Permission

The most stressful part about finding the right location is getting permission from local authorities or the property owner. Before signing any contract, make sure that you agree with the terms and conditions, such as the lease agreement, commissions payable, and legal restrictions imposed in the area. Moreover, different laws and rules apply to different vending machines, and each state may have their own specific clauses. Contact your local chamber of commerce to find out more about vending machine regulations in your area.

10 Popular Vending Machine Locations

Searching for prime locations doesn't need to be a hassle. Below is a summary of the best locations for vending machines. Take the time to research and evaluate each location to see whether it would be suitable for your business, in your specific area.

1. Apartment complexes and condos

2. Office buildings

3. Schools and universities

4. Hospitals

5. Nursing homes/care facilities

6. Car dealerships

7. Construction sites

8. Hotel and motels

9. Gyms

10. Retail stores, food courts, and shopping centers

There are vending machine locator services available for business owners. These services are run by agents who scout the city looking for the best locations for your vending machine. They take various factors into consideration, such as your monthly leasing budget, the target customers, and the types of products you sell.

One of the drawbacks with using this type of service is the large fees which are charged upfront. This makes you vulnerable to scammers who take your money but have no skill or experience in finding the right vending machine locations. Another drawback is that once they have found a list of locations, they cannot guarantee that your products will sell. Therefore, there is still a considerable amount of risk that you open yourself up to when working with a locator service.

Finding the best location on your own takes more time, but reduces a lot of risk. You will need to do most of the legwork by yourself, such as researching locations, determining the potential profits for each location, contacting owners and property managers, and following up with each lead. The benefit though is that you have more information available to decide on the best location, and you will have already established a relationship with your future landlord.

Chapter 6

Managing Your Operations

Anything that is measured and watched, improves.

–Bob Parsons

Day-to-Day Operations of a Vending Machine Business

Even though a vending machine business is considered a type of passive investment, there are minor daily tasks you will need to perform to keep your machines running smoothly. The more machines you own, the more tasks you will need to do! Fortunately, you can hire an assistant or driver to perform many of these tasks on your behalf. Below is a snapshot of the activities you will need to perform on a day-to-day basis:

- Collect products from your wholesaler or nearby storage facility.

- Check to see which items need to be restocked in your machines and plan your routes (unless you have a remote controlled machine, you may need to physically check stock levels).

- Pack your products in your delivery vehicle and head over to each machine. Refill your machines.

- Assess any wear and tear, or signs of vandalism.

Depending on how many customers purchase from your vending machine on a daily basis, you may be able to get away with refilling your machine once per week. Moreover, having an intelligent machine can save you a lot of time on reporting stock levels, calculating how much money you have earned, and other statistical and accounting information.

Software to Streamline Your Operations

If you are a serial entrepreneur or someone working at a 9-to-5 job, you won't have the luxury of time to spend on actively running your vending machine business. Fortunately, there is software on the market that can take care of many administration and process tasks on your behalf. Below is a list of popular vending machine software available on the market.

1. Quickbooks

Keep track of your business transactions and financial records with Quickbooks. It is a comprehensive accounting software that takes care of most bookkeeping tasks. Some of these tasks include calculating income and expenses, drawing monthly reports, and preparing your taxes.

2. MyVendTrack

MyVendTrack is a mobile-friendly vending route software that handles tasks like managing inventory, planning routes, calculating taxes on each machine, and doing cash readings.

3. Telemetry

Track inventory from the comfort of your home or office with Telemetry. The software tells you when your vending machine is running low on stock so you can head over and refill it.

4. VendSoft

A great all-in-one tool to use for your business is VendSoft. It has been designed to take care of management tasks and streamline the operations of your business. The software focuses on three goals: optimizing inventory, streamlining operations, and increasing business profits.

5. Seaga Smartware 360

Seaga is a vending machine manufacturer that has designed software to manage information on a machine level. For instance, the software is able to read the temperature of the machine, input calorie information for products, set product pricing, and many more features. The only drawback is that the software can only work with Seaga manufactured vending machines.

Handling the Maintenance Needs

Vending machine repair and maintenance costs can be expensive. As an operator, your main objective will be to reduce the likelihood of machine breakdowns and ensure maximum uptime. The simplest way to avoid repairs is to purchase a new machine from a reputable brand. The more reliable the brand, the better. If you are going to purchase a refurbished machine, go for the newest model that you can get. It is also important to make sure that sourcing parts for your particular model is relatively easy and inexpensive.

There are also specific ways to take care of your machine that can reduce the likelihood of maintenance work. Below are a few tips on how to look after your machine to avoid serious problems.

- When cleaning your machine, use food-grade detergent, warm water, and a soft cloth. You might need to wipe down the glass, buttons, and dollar bill validator once a week, but the machine itself only needs a clean two to three times per year.

- Position your vending machine about four inches away from the wall to ensure there is sufficient space for air to flow at the back of the machine. Overheating can lead to wear and tear, which means more frequent repair work.

- Make sure that the ground the machine is placed on is level. Uneven surfaces may lead to breakages and damage.

- If your vending machine is situated outdoors, make sure that it is not placed in direct sunlight. Too much exposure to the sun can lead to overheating and machine malfunctions.

- Double check the electrical needs of your vending machine. Look at the manual to see how much voltage it can take and make sure that the right amount of power flows. This can reduce wear and tear, as well as electrical issues or injuries.

Responding to a breakdown as soon as possible can reduce downtime and save you a lot of money. You can leave a sticker on your machine with your contact details so that customers can inform you of machine issues and other complaints immediately.

Chapter 7

Scaling vs. Growing Your Business

You don't learn to walk by following rules. You learn by doing and falling over.

–Richard Branson

Signs to Either Scale or Grow Your Business

It is every entrepreneur's dream to reach a point where they are required to expand their business. It basically means that their business has enough opportunity to make more profits! However, it is important to clarify the difference between scaling and growing a business, as these terms are typically used interchangeably.

When you grow a business, you invest more capital to expand operations, hire more people, or purchase new technologies. This is different from scaling a business, which in contrast doesn't require you to invest significantly more capital, but instead it requires you to find ways to streamline processes and be more resourceful, so you can minimize overheads and maximize revenue.

Here are common signs to look out for when it is time to scale your business:

- **You have a reliable stream of customers.** Not only does your machine attract new customers, it also draws returning customers. This has given you enough financial stability and confidence that your business can see an increase in demand in the future.

- **Your revenue has reached a plateau.** You may be breaking even or making a profit each month; however, you have noticed that there isn't a lot of cash left over after paying expenses.

- **There is a lot of room for your team to improve.** You have been fortunate enough to recruit a dynamic team, but you have not yet maximized their potential. By making a few adjustments to the workflow, you believe that you can get a lot more out of your team.

When it is time to grow your business, you will experience different kinds of problems. Here are three signs that you can look out for:

- **You have been turning down lucrative business opportunities.** Due to not having the capacity to take on more work, you have turned down a number of opportunities, such as missing out on a prime location to place an additional machine.

- **You have surpassed all of your goals.** Achieving all of your goals is a clear indication that it is time to grow your business. Failing to do so could lead to stagnancy.

- **Proven business model and reliable infrastructure.** If you have successfully established a vending machine in the right location, with the right products, and have a strong cash flow and repeat sales, then you have enough expertise and experience to rinse and repeat the concept in another location.

Of course, these signs are not a guarantee that your profitability will continue to increase; however, they are good indicators that your business is healthy enough to expand without incurring too much risk.

5 Ways to Scale Your Vending Machine Business

One of the advantages of scaling your business is that you don't have to pay an exorbitant amount of money to maximize your revenue. All that is required is a few tweaks to your systems and processes to create more income-generating opportunities. Below are five ways to scale your vending machine business.

1. Position Your Machine In Locations With High Foot Traffic

It is perfectly okay to relocate your machine once you have found a better position. When a location with high foot traffic becomes available, such as an office building, airport, or shopping mall, organize for your machine to be situated there instead. A few things that you may need to consider is your current lease agreement and the new lease that you will need to sign at the new location.

2. Switch Up or Diversify Your Products

One of the reasons why your revenue reaches a plateau is due to a decrease in demand for your products. Customers, especially those who make repeat purchases, get bored when choosing from the same selection of goods, over and over again. Switch up your catalog of products or offer niche products that take your customers by surprise! This can also be a great way to test new products that have entered the market to see how well your customers respond to them.

3. Keep Your Machine In Good Condition

An inexpensive way of scaling your business is to properly maintain your machine. This means making sure it is clean, well-stocked, and everything is functioning as it should. If you have money to spare, consider branding your machine with wrapping and signage to make it stand out from the rest of the machines within close proximity.

4. Promote Your Business on Marketing Channels

You can reach more potential customers by advertising your vending machine business on social media. Think of it like marketing any other retail business. Filter your search to look for members of your target audience within close range to your vending machine. For example, you would target people working within a business district or those who frequently visit a specific shopping mall. Take the time to build your social media presence by interacting with users, running competitions, offering coupons, and linking users to your website or blog.

5. Upgrade Your Machine

The final strategy is probably the most expensive out of them all. However, think about this way: Would you rather save costs by upgrading your machine, or spend an exorbitant amount of money buying an additional machine, paying rent for a new location, and increasing your total overheads? If you are sold on the idea of upgrading your machine, then consider buying machines with features that entice customers, such as a cashless payment system, touch screen ordering system, voice-activated customer service, and so on. The upgrade will increase revenue and keep your customer satisfaction high!

It is never advised to wait too long before you make the decision to either scale or grow your business. Ideally, you don't want to reach the point where your revenue plateaus before adjusting your processes. Bear in mind that it is not always necessary to invest more capital in your business to achieve maximum revenue. Sometimes, all it takes is finding new ways to promote your business or improving the condition of your existing machine.

Chapter 8

Laws and Regulations

Diligence is the mother of good luck.

–Benjamin Franklin

Getting the Right Paperwork for Your Business

Before you start operating your vending machine, you will need to check off a few legal requirements to keep your business in good standing. Below are some of the legal steps you will need to take to obtain the necessary licenses and permits.

Register a Legal Business Entity

The first step is to register your business. This process shouldn't take a lot of time, as long as you know what type of business structure you would like to go for. You have the option to choose between an LLC, partnership, sole proprietorship, and corporation. Each structure has its advantages and drawbacks; however, most business owners in the U.S. opt for an LLC, since it limits the owners' liability in case of lawsuits, bankruptcy, and other legal issues.

Register for Taxes

Once you have formed your company, you will need to register for federal and state taxes. The first step to do this is to apply for an EIN. The types of taxes you pay will depend on the business structure you have chosen. You can learn more about small business taxes by contacting the local IRS offices.

Open a Business Bank Account

Another way to limit your personal liability is to open a dedicated business bank account. Opening a separate bank account will also give you an opportunity to build your business credit profile, so you can gain access to business loans and other credit products.

Obtain the Necessary Permits and Licenses

Vending machine businesses who are caught operating without the necessary permits and licenses incur hefty fines, or in extreme cases, have their operations shut down. The first permit you will need to obtain is a vending machine permit. This is a requirement enforced by each state in the U.S., and must be met before the machine is situated at its location. Contact your state authorities to find out how to obtain a vending machine permit.

In addition to the permit, you will need to obtain a business license. Some of the information that is required on the business license application include:

- Federal EIN

- Sales tax number

- Beverage license (if you will be selling beverages)

- Food service license (if applicable)

- Detailed process plan about how you will install the vending machine

Once your application has been received, you will be contacted to schedule a site visit/inspection. The inspector will determine if the machine is situated in the right place and meets the local regulations.

If you are going to be selling food, you may also need to apply for a license with the local health department. They will also send an inspector to check whether or not you meet the health and hygiene regulations.

Apply for Business Insurance

Business insurance is not considered mandatory, but not getting insurance would be taking a costly risk. You want to ensure that your business profits are secure in the event of losses, injuries, or lawsuits. There are different types of insurance products to choose from, depending on your budget. The simplest and most affordable type of insurance is widely known as comprehensive business insurance.

Chapter 9

Establishing Your Team and Optimizing Customer Service

Your most unhappy customers are your greatest source of learning.

–Bill Gates

Signs to Hire Your First Employee

With the perks of semi-automated machines and vending machine software, you will be able to handle the day-to-day business tasks for the first couple of years. However, as the business grows, and you begin to manage more than one machine, managing the business alone will become strenuous. Below are some of the signs that you are ready to hire your first employee.

1. You Have Enough Work

An obvious sign of hiring someone is when you have business tasks that are too much for one person to manage. This may not be the case if you are operating a single machine, but as soon as the number of machines increases, so will the workload.

2. You Have Enough Time to Train the Employee

Hiring an employee, especially the first one to work in your company, requires a lot of commitment. You want to ensure that the employee understands your company vision and their list of duties. Most of the time, they will be representing you when you are not available to meet with suppliers and customers. Thus, it is important that you train them according to the way you would like them to perform work tasks.

3. You Can Afford To

One of the barriers to hiring someone is your company's financial stability. Some of the costs associated with recruiting an employee include:

- Recruitment costs, such as advertising, and conducting interviews and background checks.

- Employee wages, including benefits like worker's compensation.

- Unemployment and payroll taxes.

- Equipment and materials needed to perform their duties, like stationary, laptops, WiFi, telephone contract, etc.

Your company's cash flow will determine whether hiring someone is possible or not. Avoid judging your cash flow on a good month; evaluate how much money you have consistently coming in over a 12 month period. You should be able to tell if you can afford to hire someone on a contractual, freelance, part-time, or full-time basis.

Tips on Selecting the Right Employee for Your Business

As a general rule of thumb, never hire the first person you interview. Why? Because you have no one to compare them to. Unfortunately, small businesses don't have the luxury of recruiting the wrong person and starting from scratch again. The process is simply too costly to repeat unnecessarily. Therefore, when starting your search, be mindful of what you are looking for and compare candidates to find the one who best meets your criteria. Below are a few tips about finding the right employee for your business.

1. Be Clear About Your Company Vision

When you are clear about where your business is heading, and the goals you need to reach in order to achieve your vision, then finding an employee who has the capacity to assist you becomes much easier. You are able to qualify or disqualify applicants based on the type of skills and expertise you are looking for. You can also decide whether to hire someone on a part-time or full-time basis.

2. Don't Overlook Culture Fit

As important as skills are, being able to maintain a good work relationship is also vital. The type of people you recruit to your company must match the company's culture. In other words, they should share the same values as the company and be willing to adopt the company's work style. During the interview stage, you will be able to pick up on the candidate's personality and work preferences. You can also take note of how they conduct themselves and the type of work background they come from.

3. Don't Make the Decision Based on Gut Instinct

The job candidate might be charming and have an impressive résumé, but don't let their presence cloud your judgment. Before making the final decision of whether to hire the candidate or not, do a background check to make sure they are who they present themselves to be. Your background check might include calling their previous employers to verify work details, checking to see if they have a criminal record, and doing a quick Google search of their name and surname to see what comes up. If you are still not certain about the candidate, you can get a second opinion from a trusted colleague by conducting a second interview.

How to Keep Your Customers Happy and Coming Back!

The benefit of hiring an employee is that you now have someone who can interact with customers, both in person and online. You can train your employees on how to respond to customers and find new and interesting ways to keep them happy. For instance, when a customer has a complaint about your products or wants their money back, your response time should be impeccable. Below are a few strategies that you can practice (or train an employee) to increase customer satisfaction.

1. Keep the Machine Working

There is a common stereotype depicted in movies of products getting stuck inside vending machines or vending machines being out of service. Unfortunately, this stereotype has some truth to it! Far too often, customers experience problems related to purchasing goods from vending machines. You can improve customer satisfaction by simply making sure that your machine is always working. The less problems are associated with your machine, the more likely customers will recommend it to others and return to buy again.

2. Be Quick to Respond to Complaints

The shorter your response time to customers, the more likely they are to trust doing business with you. A great way to reduce response time is to apply a label on your vending machine with your business contact information written clearly. You can also include social media account handles to offer customers different communication channels.

3. Be Consistent With Refilling Your Machine

Repeat customers will likely become familiar with your refilling patterns. It is important to restock products on the same day, at the same time, to accommodate customers' buying behaviors. For example, you might have some customers who expect a certain snack in the morning or late afternoon on their commute to work or home. They would be frustrated to not find their favorite product available. For added transparency, add a label explaining which day of the week your vending machine is refilled.

4. Be Considerate of Your Customers' Preferences

You will be able to tell which products your customers love and which ones they don't seem interested in based on your inventory levels. Whenever you are purchasing new stock, be mindful of what your customers prefer to buy. There is no point in buying more products that hardly get touched. Take note of the brands, product sizes, and most in-demand items that your customers love. Every now and again, surprise them with a new product and test to see how they respond!

5. Maintain Good Relations With the Point of Contact

Even when you have an employee, there will always be someone based on the premises who is the point of contact with your customers, meaning they are likely to receive direct complaints when the machine isn't working or when customers want to find out more information. This person could be the security guard at the office building, hotel staff who hang around at the lobby, or anyone else who isn't on your payroll, but essentially represents your business. Find ways to reward this person by giving them free products or showing gratitude for the way in which they represent your business and motivate customers to return.

The co-founder of LinkedIn, Reid Hoffman said "No matter how brilliant your mind or strategy, if you're playing a solo game, you'll always lose out to a team" (Dropdesk, 2020). While it is possible—and often necessary—for startup entrepreneurs to start their businesses playing the solo game, eventually they will need to put together a team to help the business grow and keep customers happy. Finding the right people to join your company isn't as simple as vetting for skills. They also need to share the same values and passion that keep the momentum of your business going.

Chapter 10

Frequently Asked Questions (FAQs)

I knew that if I failed I wouldn't regret that, but I knew the one thing I might regret is not trying.

–Jeff Bezos

FAQs About Starting and Running a Vending Machine Business

1. Can you make a lot of money from a vending machine business?

Certainly. Vending machine businesses are profitable. However, similar to any kind of business, it takes more than a business model to make a company succeed. Some of the main factors that determine profitability for this type of business are choosing the right machine, positioning it in the right location (preferably one with a lot of foot traffic), and stocking your machine with products that customers love.

2. Do I have to pay tax on my vending machine?

Yes. Vending machine operators will be taxed on the revenue generated from each machine. The amount of sales tax payable will vary for each state. Keep an organized record of your finances to make filing taxes effortlessly.

3. What sizes do average vending machines come in?

There is no such thing as an average vending machine since they come in different options and can be customized for each business. However, if we are looking at a typical beverage machine, the average dimensions are 80" H x 40" W x 35" D. Be sure to check the size of the area before purchasing your machine.

4. How long does the process to install a vending machine take?

The time it takes to install a vending machine depends on the supplier. However, on average it can take 15–20 days for your machine to be installed from the day you make a deposit or full payment, to the day it arrives on the premises.

5. Can vending machines be rented out?

Of course, there are businesses across the country who lease vending machines, or offer a rent-to-buy agreement. This may be an affordable option if you don't have a lot of startup capital but are not prepared to downgrade on the type and model of your vending machine.

6. What type of electrical outlet do I need to run my machine?

Most vending machines use 115 volts at 10–12 amps to operate. This means that you need a standard three-prong outlet to power your machine.

7. What can I do if my vending machine is vandalized?

It can be upsetting to find your vending machine vandalized. Not only does this affect your business by causing downtime, but it can also set you back financially. The best way to protect your business against vandalism is to install cameras on the machine or nearby, ensure that the location has 24/7 security, and most of all—get yourself covered with insurance.

8. How many product slots does an average vending machine have?

While vending machines vary in how they are designed, a standard snack and beverage machine has about 8–10 slots to insert products. Note that the sizes of the slots can be different for each machine.

9. How much commission will I need to pay the property owner where my machine is situated?

Not every property will charge a commission for placing your machine on their premises. For some owners, they regard your vending machine as free marketing to lure customers into their property. However, you may get owners who want a commission from your profits. This could range between 0–20% of net profit. The commission and other terms of trade can be negotiated, and will appear on your signed contract.

10. If I want to purchase an existing vending machine business, how do I get access to that information?

The best place to search for vending machine business for sale is online. Look for online marketplaces that specifically deal with selling businesses. As part of your background check and screening of potential companies, contact the following state resources:

- Federal Trade Commission (1-877-382-4357)

- National Fraud Information (1-800-876-7060)

- Small Business Association (1-800-U-ASK-SBA)

- Better Business Bureau (www.bbb.org)

Conclusion

Starting and running a vending machine is not a walk in the park, but neither is starting any kind of business. Nevertheless, when compared to other startups, particularly those in the food and retail industry, a vending machine business is what I would call startup-friendly.

If you have never previously run a business before, or perhaps have too much on your plate to actively manage a business, then this low-maintenance and semi-automated business is for you!

Most of the time, money, and effort you will need to invest will be upfront. But once you have the legal paperwork sorted, location locked, and vending machine purchased, the only major work you will need to do is restock your machine with products and count all of the money you will be making!

The best time to have started a vending machine business was yesterday because, truth be told, the competition in this market is incredibly tight! However, today is also a good day to get started on setting up your business.

This blueprint has been designed to give you the framework for running a successful vending machine business. You will need to do your part and research which strategies will work for you and your specific business model. Don't be afraid to do the work—it will eventually pay off!

If you have found this blueprint valuable, kindly leave a review.

References

Blomquist, C. (2014, March 1). 3 Easy steps to keep customers happy and achieve booming vending machine sales. Parlevel Systems. https://www.parlevelsystems.com/2014/03/01/the-customer-experience/

Burnwal, K. (2020, June 4). Day-to-day operations to run a vending business. Wendor. https://wendor.in/day-to-day-operations-to-run-vending-machine-business/

CorpNet. (n.d.). Process paperwork for a vending machine and device permit. CorpNet. https://www.corpnet.com/business-licenses/vending-machine-and-device-permit/

Darlington, N. (2022, October 17). Time to hire your first employee? 5 Signs to watch for. FreshBooks Blog. https://www.freshbooks.com/blog/hire-your-first-employee?fb_dnt=1

Dropdesk. (2020, August 3). 101 Inspirational quotes for startups. The DropDesk Blog. https://drop-desk.com/blog/startup-quotes

Gleeson, P. (2019, March 1). Vending machine business pros and cons. Chron.com. https://smallbusiness.chron.com/vending-machine-business-pros-cons-1363.html

Grand View Research. (2019). Vending machine market size and share. Grandviewresearch.com. https://www.grandviewresearch.com/industry-analysis/global-vending-machine-market

Hassler, L. (n.d.). 5 Clear signs that now is time to scale your business. YourBizRules. https://www.yourbizrules.com/5-clear-signs-scale-your-business/

Hovis, T. (2017, August 18). 3 Ways to stand out in the vending industry with remarkable customer service. Cantaloupe. https://www.cantaloupe.com/3-ways-to-stand-out-in-the-vending-industry-with-remarkable-customer-service/

IBISWorld. (2022, May 31). Vending machine operators in the US - Market size 2005–2028. Www.ibisworld.com. https://www.ibisworld.com/industry-statistics/market-size/vending-machine-operators-united-states/

Keninsights. (2022, August 7). 8 Ways to scale your vending business to 6 figure business. Keninsights. https://www.keninsights.com/8-ways-to-scale-your-vending-business-to-6-figure-business/

Lavinsky, D. (2021, December 26). Vending machine business plan template [updated 2022]. Growthink. https://www.growthink.com/businessplan/help-center/vending-machine-business-plan

Logic Vending. (2018, December 10). The ultimate guide to purchasing a vending machine. Logic Vending.

https://www.logicvending.co.uk/guide-purchasing-vending-machine

Measom, C. (2021, May 17). How to start a vending machine business: Costs, pros and cons. GOBankingRates. https://www.gobankingrates.com/money/business/how-to-start-a-vending-machine-business/

Nazar, J. (2013, September 9). 16 Surprising statistics about small businesses. Forbes. https://www.forbes.com/sites/jasonnazar/2013/09/09/16-surprising-statistics-about-small-businesses/?sh=62f1115b5ec8

NerdWallet. (2021, March 31). How to start a vending machine business: Cost, tips, pros and cons. NerdWallet. https://www.nerdwallet.com/article/small-business/how-to-start-a-vending-machine-business#:~:text=With%20as%20little%20as%20a

Papich, T. (2022, August 2). Best products for your vending machines. EVending. https://www.evending.com/best-products-for-your-vending-machines/

TCN Vending. (2021, July 16). Vending machine near me: How to find the right location. TCN Vending. https://www.tcnvending.com.au/blog/vending-machine-near-me/

Tomasso, C. (n.d.). List of vending machine software. Vendinghow.com. https://vendinghow.com/article/vending-machine-software

Truic Team. (2020, October 19). How to start a vending machine business. HowToStartAnLLC.com. https://howtostartanllc.com/business-ideas/vending-machine

VendSoft. (n.d.-a). Buying supplies for your vending machine business. Www.vendsoft.com. https://www.vendsoft.com/buying-supplies-vending-machine-business/

VendSoft. (n.d.-b). Can software make your vending machine business more successful? - VendSoft. Www.vendsoft.com. https://www.vendsoft.com/software-makes-vending-business-successful/

VendSoft. (n.d.-c). Reduce the chance of vending machine repair needs. Www.vendsoft.com. https://www.vendsoft.com/vending-machine-repair/

VenTech Media. (2020, March 30). Are vending machines profitable? Naturals2Go. https://www.naturals2go.com/are-vending-machine-profitable/#:~:text=The%20typical%20vending%20machine%20generates